40 Mistakes I Made During 30 Years As a Landlord

Category:	Business & Economics
ID:	26175234
ISBN:	978-1-67810-824-3
Copyright:	2020
License:	Standard Copyright License
Language:	English
Country:	United States
Published by	Lulu Publishing
Author	Bob Oros

I0479678

Description: If you own any number of rental properties, or you are thinking of investing in some, let this book be your guide and help you avoid the many costly mistakes that are inevitable. The solutions to these 40 mistakes were discovered over a 30 year period through trial and error. You can avoid them all and save many discouraging hours by knowing how to deal with tenants and rental property.

Key words: landlord, landlord mistakes, landlord FAQ, evicting tenants, renting a property, renting to family, buying rental properties, rental deposits, land trust, collecting overdue rent, rental agreement, mistakes landlords make, returning rent deposits, rental agreement termination,

ISBN 978-1-67810-824-3

9 781678 108243

90000

Contents

About the author

Bob Oros has been a self employed full time sales trainer since 1992 with over 2,000 speaking engagements in all 50 states and several international locations. Due to being self employed, Bob did not have a company retirement plan and started buying rental properties to compensate.

Since real estate was a sideline business he did not have the expertise to deal with the many problems that came up. Having no one to turn to for advise, he had to learn everything the hard way.

If you own any number of rental properties, or you are thinking of investing is some, let Bob be your guide and help you avoid the many costly mistakes that are inevitable.

1. How do I buy a property?

Ninety-five percent of the people buying real estate investment courses and attend seminars never buy their first property.

Why? Fear of the unknown. Fear of making a mistake. It is easy to understand why most folks never take the first step even though it can be the most profitable investment they ever make.

Here are a few mistakes I made on my first purchases.

On the house I was buying, I was more concerned about being approved by the lender rather than focusing on what I was buying. It must have been because I was buying it for a rental property and using an 80/20 loan. I was buying it for an investment property, and the bank knew it. It's just that I borrowed the 20% down from the same bank, and I was worried about getting the loan.

They were selling through a broker, and she was suspicious of my motive. The loan had nothing to do with her, and she didn't know how I was financing the property. This rattled my confidence and made me overlook some important issues.

Many borrowers intentionally misrepresented their living situation in order to secure a smaller down payment and lower interest rates for their loan. But misleading your lender about owner occupancy is an incredibly risky move. Lying on a mortgage application is considered mortgage fraud and is illegal.

In addition, penalties for mortgage fraud – which is what lies on a mortgage application is – range as high as 30 years in prison and a $1 million fine. You likely won't face a penalty like that for a small exaggeration or omission, but you could still end up with a fine and a conviction.

I did buy other houses and actually moved in and stayed for a couple of years before moving out, renting it, then buying another. This is perfectly legitimate.

If I had it to do over again here is what I would do.

First, I would have put the broker in her place. After all, she is just an overpaid service provider with no skin in the game. I try to avoid them at all cost. Six percent is an outrageous amount of commission to pay for services that any good mortgage broker can provide at no cost. They just clutter up the sale. The seller is paying, but in the end, the buyer pays. More about brokers as we go forward.

Second, I let the broker pick the inspector. Huge mistake. I think the guy did a drive-by inspection.

After the closing I had my insurance give me a quote. He wouldn't approve the roof! The furnace had a crack in the heat exchanger. I was so mad I took the furnace out myself, ordered a new one wholesale and put it in myself. I discovered it was not that hard. I had a heat and air guy come and hook it up.

There was a roofing job going on down the street and I asked the crew foreman to stop by my house after he was done for the day. I bypassed the contractor, bought the shingles at Home Depot and had them put on a new roof. I was shocked to learn how much the contractor makes! I saved at least 50%, but I shouldn't have had to do it in the first place.

This is risky because in some states you must hire a licensed contractor. However, in Oklahoma, you do not need a license to be a contractor. It is still risky because you are doing it without insurance. I don't recommend it.

If I would have been smart, I would have had the seller make those repairs before the closing. That's what I want you to do. Buy it right.

Another mistake I made was paying what they were selling it for. Why? As I said, I was worried about getting the mortgage. I was buying it on an 80/20 with no out of pocket money and I was self-employed. And I wanted it. I should have been more willing to walk.

More tips about buying as we go forward. But for now, the big lesson is you are the one with the money. You are the one signing the 20 or 30-year mortgage. You are the one who has to live with the property. In a way, it's like a marriage. You have to date before you jump in. Same with a property. Inspect, inspect, inspect. Ask tough questions. Be bold. Buying is not a personality contest where you want everyone to like you.

So, when buying, act like a buyer! Be tough! Ask for everything. It's all about attitude and getting what you want.

You have to display an attitude of confidence when you invest in a rental property. This is not the time to take a "hat-in-hand" approach. After all, you are making a huge investment and one small mistake can cost you a bunch of money.

I kept this house for several years. I made a small profit every month and as the years went by I increased the rent so it was making a decent profit. The value increased I refinanced my first and second mortgage into a single loan. I kept it well maintained and my last tenants stayed for nearly 8 years. They not only paid the rent every month, they actually paid it 2 months in advance. They eventually bought the property and I received a huge paycheck.

I made some additional improvements over the years including new floors, remodeling the kitchen ceiling, building a gazebo in the backyard for a hot tub, a new fence and painting the entire house.

2. What about home inspectors?

What is a home inspection?

A home inspection is an objective visual examination of the physical structure and systems of a house, from the roof to the foundation.

What does a home inspection include?

The Inspector does not evaluate whether or not you're getting good value for your money. Generally, an inspector checks (and gives prices for repairs on): the electrical system, plumbing and waste disposal, the water heater, insulation and Ventilation, the HVAC system, water source and quality, the potential presence of pests, the foundation, doors, windows, ceilings, walls, floors, and roof. Be sure to hire a home inspector that is qualified and experienced.

It's a good idea to have an inspection before you sign a written offer since, once the deal is closed, you've bought the house as is." Or, you may want to include an inspection clause in the offer when negotiating for a home. An inspection t clause gives you an 'out" on buying the house if serious problems are found, or gives you the ability to renegotiate the purchase price if repairs are needed. An inspection clause can also specify that the seller must fix the problems before you purchase the house.

The American Society of Home Inspectors (ASHI) publishes a Standards of Practice and Code of Ethics that outlines what you should expect to be covered in your home inspection report.

Home inspectors are a seller's worst nightmare and a buyer's best friend. A good one can save you thousands of dollars when buying.

I bought one house and after learning some hard lessons I played the game with a whole different set of rules.

This was a house I was going to live in. Before I started looking I refinanced my first two properties and came up with a 20% down payment. On a personal residence, you cannot only get a really good interest rate with a 20% down payment, but you don't have to pay a PMI, private mortgage insurance.

In case you are not familiar with PMI, it is the fee that FHA, Fannie May or the VA charge to ensure the bank's risk on the amount above 80%.

Having a 20% down payment and a preapproved mortgage puts you in a completely different frame of mind. Instead of being a timid buyer with a broker controlling the deal, I was now a highly confident buyer ready to rattle the seller's broker's cage.

A well-prepared buyer is a broker's second worst nightmare. The first nightmare is a buyer with their own inspector. When she tried to recommend her inspector I confidently told her I had my own. I could see the fear in her eyes. I know what she was thinking. *"How could a meager home buyer have their own inspector? They are supposed to use the inspector I recommend so the sale will go through without a hitch. How dare this guy put my commission in jeopardy."*

After doing a little research I found a home inspector that was as thorough and professional as anyone I have ever met.

Here's what he did.

He found hail damage on the roof and gutters. My inspector looked under the furnace and found the walls of the underground vents had some serious problems. They were rusted and sand was partially blocking the airflow.

Further investigation revealed that there had been dampness in the floor vents. He also discovered that on one side of the house the yard slopped and rainwater flowed towards the house causing the problem with the underground vents. He also discovered the bottom of the garbage disposal was rusted. The dishwasher was not working correctly and to top it all off, the garage door had some problems.

Here's the deal. Once these problems are revealed the seller is required by law to make them know to potential buyers before selling the house. It's called a residential property condition disclosure statement.

I ended up buying it with a new roof, new gutters, new garage door and opener, yard leveled so water would drain away from the house including a French drain, a new heating system with overhead ducts, new garbage disposal and a new dishwasher.

I lived in the house for 3 years, rented it out for 3 years, and ended up selling it.

I made some mistakes when I sold the house that we will discuss later so you can avoid them.

3. Should you use a broker?

Real estate agents can be helpful when you're buying or selling a home. Real estate agents can provide you with information on homes and neighborhoods that isn't easily accessible to the public. Their knowledge of the home buying process, negotiating skills, and familiarity with the area you want to live in can be extremely valuable.

Brokers can work independently or employ other agents. The biggest difference between the titles is a broker can work on his own, while an agent must work under a licensed broker. A real estate associate broker is an agent that's working on a broker's license.

There are so many types of real estate agents that even agents sometimes confuse themselves. Some agents add titles after their names to help them stand out in a crowd. They might be associates, real estate consultants, salesperson, or REALTOR, but they all must be licensed to sell real estate.

Real estate brokers can work as agents but agents can't work as brokers, at least not without a broker's license. Agents who give real estate advice must have a real estate license. Most states maintain an online site where consumers can look up an agent's name, get a license number, and check on any violations filed against him.

What exactly is a real estate broker?

A real estate broker is a step above a real estate agent. A broker generally has more education than an agent, but not always. A real estate broker can work independently or hire real estate salespersons. The exact rules can vary from state to state, but most have somewhat similar requirements.

What Is a Broker Associate?

A broker associate is a real estate broker who works for another real estate broker. Although the broker could work for himself, many choose to join a larger real estate network. Some pay a flat fee to the employing broker and some earn a percentage of each transaction.

What Is a Real Estate Agent?

Agents are licensed salespeople. They're not real estate brokers. A real estate agent must work for an employing broker and cannot work independently. Brokers are responsible for their real estate agents' actions.

What Is a REALTOR®?

A REALTOR® can be a real estate broker or a real estate agent. All REALTORS® are agents or brokers, but not all agents or brokers are REALTORS®. It's a title that means the individual belongs to the National Association of REALTORS® (NAR), subscribes to its extensive Code of Ethics, and pays annual dues. Not every real estate agent belongs to NAR.

What Is a Listing Agent?

Listing agents are also known as seller's agents because they represent the seller. A listing agent can be a real estate broker or a real estate agent. These types of agents have a responsibility to the seller under a listing agreement and must protect that interest.

What Is a Buyer's Agent?

A buyer's agent is known as a selling agent, not be confused with a seller's agent, a buying agent or, in some states, an exclusive buyer's agent.

Exclusive buyer's agents never work for sellers. Many agents, however, work with both sellers and buyers, although not usually in the same transaction. Buyer's agents might or might not require a buyer to sign a buyer's broker agreement, depending on local custom and law.

What Is a Transaction Agent?

In states where dual agency is not permitted, listing agents might find themselves in the position of writing an offer for the buyer. These agents can elect to become transaction agents. He doesn't represent either party but simply facilitates the transaction.

How do Real Estate Commissions work?

Real estate commissions are often shared among many people. In a typical real estate transaction, the commission might be split four ways:

Listing agent – the agent who took the listing from a seller

Listing broker – the broker for whom the listing agent works

Buyer's agent – the agent who represents the buyer

For example, let's assume an agent takes a listing on a $200,000 house at a 6% commission rate. The house sells for the asking price, and the listing broker and the buyer's agent's broker each get half of the commission, or $6,000 each ($200,000 sales price x 0.06 commission ÷ 2). The brokers then split the commissions with the agents. A common commission split gives 60% to the agent and 40% to the broker, but the split could be 50/50, 60/40, 70/30, or whatever ratio the agent and broker have agreed upon. In a

60/40 split, each agent in our example would receive $3,600 ($6,000 X 0.6), and each broker would keep $2,400 ($6,000 X 0.4). The final commission breakdown would be:

Listing agent - $3,600
Listing broker - $2,400
Buyer's agent - $3,600
Buyer's agent's broker - $2,400

Sometimes commissions are split among fewer parties. If a broker lists a property and then finds a buyer, for instance, he or she would keep the full 6% (or other agreed-upon rates) commission. Or, if a listing agent also sells the property (acting as both listing agent and buyer's agent), he or she would split the commission only with his or her sponsoring broker. If the commission were $12,000 as in the previous example, the broker would keep $4,800 and the agent would receive $7,200, assuming the same 60/40 split.

Their earnings are often eroded by taxes and business expenses. Federal, state and self-employment taxes, along with the costs of doing business (insurance, dues, and fees, MLS fees, advertising, etc.), can end up taking sizable chunks out of otherwise substantial commissions. All paid by you, the seller.

What should I ask a real estate agent?

1. What experience do you have?

2. What's your marketing plan?

3. How will you keep me informed of your progress?

4. What's your commission?

5. Do you have references you can give me?

Be certain to get the names of recent clients. It's always helpful for the broker to have a page or two of quotes from clients for that first meeting, but don't rely solely on that. Make the calls.

Example of an interview.

An open house is a perfect way to interview a potential agent. I recently visited an open house and talked with the listing agent. She was a dental assistant trying to break into real estate sales. I realize everyone has to start somewhere and this might be fine for someone who doesn't have a clue about how to sell a house. But for an investor, it would be better to learn how to bypass the real estate agents. If you were going to hire someone to sell your house worth $200,000 you would want to do some serious interviews. I eliminated her with question number one.

Here's an example from my neighborhood.

I was acquainted with an older couple who lived three houses down from one of my rental properties. Her husband passed away and the house was too much for her to take care of. I knew the value of the home to be around $140,000. I assumed she would get an offer close to that number. She really needed the money to pay for her retirement expenses.

A few weeks after her house went on the market, I called the number on the for sale sign to see what was going on. The real estate salesperson was excited to tell me that he sold the house within a week of listing it. I asked him how much it sold for and this is what he told me.

"I wanted to make a quick sale so we lowered the price to $120,000 and it sold in 7 days." The owner didn't want a quick sale. Sure, she could have said no, but try telling that to a salesperson who works on commission.

This woman needed all the money she could get for the house. The salesperson took $20,000 out of her equity and basically gave it away. The seller had to pay 6% commission divided up between the broker, the listing agent, and the selling agent. That was another $7,200 for a total of $27,200.

That is the way the real estate business works mostly because there are so many people trying to sell houses for a living. **The National Association of Realtors reported 87% of all new agents fail after five years in the industry and only 13% make it**. Agents don't leave the industry because they made too much money, no, they leave the industry because they didn't make any.

The 2% technique. Here's how it works.

The listing salesperson comes in and says he or she will sell your house for a 2% commission. You think, "wow, this is great!" What they neglect to tell you is that is IF they personally sell it. Since that very rare, if ever happens, you have to still pay the seller's 3%, which is again split with the big guy broker. So you end up paying 5% and the listing salesperson takes his 2% for doing nothing except putting your house on the MLS at a cost of about $100 for some starving selling real estate salesperson to sell to one of his or her family members. It is most likely the only sale the selling salesperson will ever make because they quit the business and you will never hear from them again.

Here is a method to save 3% of the value of your property. Put a "For Sale By Owner" sign in front of your property.

If it was you selling the house and you didn't want to bother with it, but you didn't want to pay 6%, here's what I would recommend. Go to Home Depot, buy a For Sale By Owner sign and put it in front of your house.

The real estate people would be on your doorstep within 24 hours. All you would have to say is "bring me a buyer with a good offer and I will pay you 3% commission." Then wait until you get 3 offers and go with the highest one. They are now competing for the sale.

I recently put a property up for sale as a for sale by owner. I sold it without a listing or selling real estate salesperson within 2 days for my asking price. More on that later.

I think the real estate profession is a good career and there are plenty of excellent real estate companies out there who fill a need.

For you, an investor, it's best to learn how to put some of that available commission in your pocket.

4. Mistakes to avoid making an offer.

The appraiser is the one who determines the price. The way he does it is by using "comps" or recent comparable sales in the area.

You could have two houses side by side. One is remodeled and has a new heat and air system, new roof and landscaping. The other one is the original heat and air, in need of a new roof and in need of cosmetic updates. They will more than likely appraise for the same price. The appraiser is only interested in the price per square foot for the most recent sales. This is true in most areas of the country unless the market is favoring buyers due to few homes on the market.

Start to think in terms of price per square foot. Here is an example.

The above shows the date it was actually sold, the address, the selling price, the number of square feet and the price per square foot. Now we have a number to work with. $86.73 per square foot. This information is readily available on the county's website. Just look up the taxes on a property, then click a little deeper until you come to a link that says "subdivision sales". You will find a list of homes sold in that subdivision dating back several years. Click on each individual property and you will find the square feet.

Our goal is to find a home like the one we described above that is in need of repair. Take the square foot and multiply it by the average addition price per square foot.

Let's say it's 1500 SF. The average per SF addition price is $87. That comes to $130,500.

Next, you start deducting the cost of repairs. Let's estimate the total cost to bring it up to a market price is $30,500. We make a list of the necessary repairs to take to the selling salesperson.

We are now at a $100,000 offer. But wait! There are two more factors. These are most important because you probably knew everything so far.

Don't buy it unless there is an opportunity to increase the square footage. Let's say there is a breezeway between the house and the garage that can be closed in and the walls covered with sheetrock, a window installed at one end and perhaps a door at the other end. You put down laminate flooring or tile and make it into a great looking room. Let's say it's 8' by 16'. The SF of the house just went from 1500 SF to 1628 SF. An increase of 128 SF multiplied by $87 per

SF. The value just increased by $11,136 with an investment of less than one thousand dollars.

The next thing to look for is how the seller is determining the total SF. If they have not had an actual appraisal, and are using the SF based on the county records, the SF is going to be grossly under the appraisers SF. This is true in most cases, not all. Don't ask me why, but very few people know this.

When the appraiser does his work, all he will say is yep! It will appraise at the price you are selling it for. He may not even look at the county records. It doesn't happen that way all the time, but for the most part it does.

So if you pick up another 200 SF from the new appraisal (which you are paying for as the buyer) another $17,400 added to the value.

I get postcards and letters in the mail from people wanting to buy my properties. When I call them for a price, they offer 70% of the market value less any repairs. Who wouldn't want to buy property at that price? I guess there are desperate people who are willing to give away their equity to get out from under some kind of mess they are in.

If you can do it by adding SF and finding a discrepancy on the county records, you can increase the value enough to refinance, do the repairs that are needed, and have a nice, long term investment. If you know how to deal with tenants, they will pay off your mortgage while appreciation is increasing the value even more.

On one of my "keeper" houses, I have a tenant who is a beautician. She was cutting hair in the living room. I said why don't I build on a beauty parlor for you. She thought I was the greatest landlord on the planet. I enclosed the breezeway as we discussed above, hooked up a sink and some extra outlets, and she had a really nice place to bring her customers. She will be there a long time. I give her 2 receipts so she can deduct the shop rent. One for $400 for the shop and one for $1100 for the rent.

But the thing to keep in mind is the value of the house, based on SF, went up by over $11,000 by adding on the room. It cost me about $500 to add the room.

When making an offer, think "square feet."

5. How to choose a mortgage lender.

His name is Brett Baldwin. He is the Branch Manager for Gateway Mortgage Group here in Oklahoma City.

Here is an example of what a really good mortgage professional can do.

Friday afternoon I put my For Sale By Owner sign in the front yard of the property. I also had a sign by each entrance of the sub division. I started to get some calls from real people, not real estate salespeople looking for a listing.

On Saturday morning I had an interested buyer. He and his wife came back for a second look in the afternoon and to take some measurements. They decided to buy it at one of the three prices I offered. (More on my three prices later).

I sent Brett a text letting him know they would be calling.

They called Brett late Saturday evening. Brett got all the information, had them fill out an application online, and got them approved.

Sunday he emailed them the contract. They printed it at their home and dropped it off at my house.

I reviewed the contract, signed it, and dropped it off at Brett's office Monday morning.

The deal is done, the house is sold. All that was left was to wait on the closing company.

Compare that to a real estate salesperson. They are just not equipped to get things done that fast. They basically do the leg work that you can do.

If you are going to be buying and selling, it is really necessary to learn how to bypass the broker.

6. What about my credit score?

This is a big problem that most beginners in real estate investment and home buyers have when trying to make deals work. They simply do not know what their credit rating is, and therefore do not understand what type of loan programs and financing they can use. In real estate, your number one asset is your credit. Without it, it is extremely hard to get a purchase to go through—although it can be possible! Having bad credit really does make things harder than they should be.

But realistically, more people than ever before seem to have some type of credit problem. However, with a plan you can improve your credit score and achieve your real estate goals.

Bad credit and bankruptcy are two very common issues a lot of people have questions about when they begin to think about buying a home or an investment property. Both bad credit and bankruptcy will be red flags to some lenders, and they may put you in a very high interest rate category for any loans that you may qualify for. That's part of the deal you get stuck with if your credit is not so good. But, you still can get help; it will just take a bit more effort and determination on your part.

Your credit score is like the dreaded report card you got when you were in school. Following is a summary of the different levels of a credit score.

589-480 – Bad (C credit)

Usually signifies MANY significant (60 days or more) late payments on a mortgage loan in prior 2 years and widespread MAJOR (60-90 DAYS) late on credit payments in prior 3 years. People with C credit typically will receive higher rates and higher required equity or down payment on all loan types, except government loans (FHA and VA) which will not rely solely on credit scoring. Examples of "C" credit include a middle or average credit score of 520 to 580 or worse; in most cases a score of 520 is the cutoff for APPROVAL from PORTFOLIO loan buyers whose loans are equity driven.

Bankruptcies must be discharged at the time of loan application to qualify as having "Poor" credit. Current charge offs, bad debts and judgments sometimes need not be paid off to get a mortgage. The penalty is a reduced pool of lenders, higher rates, and stiff prepayment penalties if you refinance within 3 years.

Credit scoring will place borrowers in one of three general categories.

1. A borrower with a score at 680 and above may be considered an A+ loan. The loan will involve basic underwriting, probably through a "computerized automated underwriting" system and be completed within minutes. Borrowers

2. A score below 680 but above 620 may indicate lenders will take a closer look at the file in determining potential

risks. Borrowers falling in this category may find the process and underwriting time no different than the past.

3. Borrowers with a score below 620 may find themselves locked out of the best loan rates and terms offered by lenders. Mortgage professionals may divert these borrowers to alternate funding sources other than FNMA and FHLMC.

If you do not currently own your own home because of some credit problems or because you believe your income is not big enough to make payments, there is still a way you can get into a house.

HUD plays a large role in homeownership by making loans available for lower-and moderate-income families through its FHA mortgage insurance program and its HUD Homes program. HUD owns homes in many communities throughout the U.S. and offers them for sale at attractive prices and economical terms.

FHA, a division of HUD, works to make homeownership a possibility. With the FHA, you don't need perfect credit or a high-paying job to qualify for a loan. The FHA also makes loans more accessible by requiring smaller down payments than conventional loans. In fact, an FHA down payment could be as little as a few months' rent. And your monthly payments may not be much more than rent.

Anyone who meets the credit requirements can afford the mortgage payments and cash investment, and who plans to use the mortgaged property as a primary residence may apply for an FHA insured loan.

7. How many properties do you need?

The first step is, of course, to buy your own home. You will immediately begin to take advantage of the monthly appreciation and mortgage reduction.

There are very few investments that will give you a good return and at the same time provide you with a place to live.

Once you own your home and if time is on your side you can simply buy ONE additional single family home and pay it off over the next 20 or 30 years. The principle and income you would receive from that single investment would equal an entire lifetime of working at a job and receiving a pension.

By simply owning one additional $150,000 home you would double your yearly appreciation from $4,000 to $8,000 as well as pay down the mortgage balance. Even if the rent only covered your principle, interest, taxes and insurance, you are more than making it up on the mortgage pay down and the property appreciation. Plus there is a tax advantage.

As time went on the rent would eventually increase you the one rental property would begin to pay the mortgage on your personal house.

This approach takes a lot of the pressure off that many people feel when they think they have to be a landlord with a lot of problem tenants. All you have to look for is one.

This is a crucial point in your program for investing in real estate. Many people take the option of simply upgrading to a bigger home. This is a perfectly logical thing to do for people who have a sound career and are sure of their company retirement program. Once you move from a conservative home to a larger one, there is no going back. Until, that is, you are living in a million dollar home and will be okay with selling it and downgrading to a smaller place along with your MBA Massive Bank Account. Before making that choice it is always a good idea to examine all your options and your long range goals.

There are three milestones you should consider.

The first milestone is to own one personal home and three nearby rental properties. The amount of work required to maintain three rentals is not that difficult. You can keep them until you retire, and depending on your age, you will have a really good income to subsidize your social security and company pension.

The second milestone is four to ten properties. This is the growing period for an investor. It is especially good for someone like a plumber, carpenter, electrician, salesperson or handyman who doesn't have a 9 to 5 job that requires being present during those hours. If you work in the surrounding area you are available for issues that will arise.

I fell into this category. Except I had to travel for my business. I was an independent sales trainer and had to travel all over the country to serve my clients. Even with this situation, I was able to manage my properties without much problem. The reason I tell you that is you can do it as well.

The next milestone is ten or more. This is when you are considered a real estate investor. You can usually hire someone to take care of maintenance issues which frees you up to pursue other interests or to keep adding to your portfolio. Or, you can do as many people do, and that is to quit your full time job and become your own handyman or handywoman.

8. Where to buy your property?

This is really important.

It's Friday evening and you are just getting ready to sit down and watch a movie. The phone rings and your tenant's garage door won't open. It's a simple thing, the door's safety device is out of line keeping the door from opening. A five-minute fix.

If the house is in the neighborhood travel time is 5 minutes. If it's on the other side of town, your evening is shot due to the Friday evening traffic you have to deal with. That's why this is important.

This seems to be a huge mistake many investors make. One of the first questions I always ask fellow investors is where are your rental properties. They frown and tell me they are in a nearby town. This normally happens because they got a good deal on the property.

Another personal preference is buying in a low-end neighborhood. Even though the cash flow potential is usually greater, this is offset by the type of tenants you end up with. If you have to make a repair at 10:00 PM, would you feel safe? You just never know what a tenant might call you about.

I always keep my properties well protected against bugs and pests. However, one night at 11:00 PM one of my single mom tenants called me in a panic. There was a dead mouse on the kitchen floor! Just think if I had to go across town to pick up a dead mouse and put it in the trash. But the house was one block away. Within 15 minutes the task was done and I was back In bed.

Another personal rule I have always had is never to buy a house that you wouldn't personally live in. You just never know what might happen and if the chips were down you could pick one of your rentals, sell off all the others and have a place to live that is paid for.

Buying in your own addition also gives you up to date information, because you are there every day. Every time you drive out of the neighborhood you can go by your property to make sure everything looks okay or to make sure there is nothing going on.

Every time a for sale sign goes up, or a for rent sign suddenly appears, you can make a call get up to the minute market information.

I recently went to an open house. I was simply driving by and the time was between the open house hours so I stopped. The house looked great, however, the price was really high! I came home and told my wife. We agreed the house would never sell. The next day I drove by and there was a big, bold sold sign across the original sign. When you own several properties in the neighborhood and you just found out the price per square foot just went up by $5.00, you can imagine how good that makes you feel. At the time I owned 14,000 square feet in the neighborhood. Five dollars times 14,000 square feet is a mighty good increase - $70,000! Unlike most types of investments, you are in 100% control of your property.

When I was at my peak of ownership I could easily walk to every property I owned. Three or four days a week I would go for a walk and add up my assets of well over a million dollars'.

I used to think, "If I did nothing for the next 10 years, the houses would be paid way down, the value would go way up and I would be very comfortable." Bottom line. It did and I am, and so can you.

9. What about a Land Trust.

Everything I owned was in a land trust. Here's why:

Individuals use land trusts for privacy and to avoid probate. Many investors buy properties through land trusts to prevent their names appearing in public records. The land trust also allows the property to immediately pass to the owner's heirs upon death, rather than go through a lengthy probate process.

Some of the other advantages of land trusts for individuals are:

Sales price of the property can be kept off the public records.

Property taxes are lower if the purchase price is kept private.

Judgments or liens (such as IRS liens) against an individual's name are not a lien against their land trust property.

Partners can more easily continue a project if one dies or is divorced.

Interests can be transferred quickly without recording a deed.

Managing a rental property is easier when the trustee can be used as a "bad guy.".

Negotiating a purchase or sale can be easier when the trustee can be used.

Liability on financing can be limited to the assets of the trust.

Lease options can be placed into a trust, with the purchaser recording the option.

Make loans "Assumable-like" by using a land trust. Transferring title into a land trust with the seller as beneficiary does not usually trigger the due-on-sale clause of the mortgage holder.

The above is basically my opinion based on my personal experience. I would advise you to learn everything you can about a land trust, do everything yourself if you have time to figure it all out, then have it checked by an attorney.

10. What about insurance?

Your main concern when it comes to insuring rental properties will be the structure including the roof and foundation and other buildings on the premises. Ask your agent about options regarding multi-family dwellings if you're insuring an apartment, condo, or duplex.

No matter what kind of property you're renting out and regardless of to whom and when, there are a few key things to think about when it comes to insuring any rental property.

1. Furnishing appliances with the property.

When you rent out a home, an apartment, a condo or any other structure to a third party, you need to insure the property itself, but you're not required to insure the contents. The exception to this would be any appliances you are leaving in the property – a dishwasher, stove, refrigerator or washer and dryer, for example. The standard fire policy for rental homes doesn't automatically include coverage for them, and you need coverage specifically for those items. Figure out how much it would cost to replace them all at once, and make sure that's the minimum amount you have for personal property coverage.

Contents belonging to the tenants will be their responsibility. Have a conversation with your tenants urging them to buy a renter's insurance policy to indemnify them if they experience a loss of contents. If a fire or storm destroys the home and contents inside, your insurance will not pay out if their possessions are damaged or destroyed.

2. Protecting rental income.

One important factor regarding your insurance coverage is deciding whether you want to have insurance for the income you make from renting.

If a fire or storm damage makes the home unlivable, your tenants will be finding alternate housing. Until they come back or until the house can be re-rented, you won't be receiving rental income during that time. If you ask for rental income protection on your insurance, payments can be made to make up that gap.

Your insurance policy can cover fair rental value in the event of a loss. You'll have to decide how much you'd receive in annual rental income and obtain insurance for that amount. This is vital if your budget is greatly dependent on rental income and if finances are tight. Having a mortgage to pay without the rental income to support it could cause you to lose your property.

3. Maximizing your profit from rental income by making smart insurance choices.

Of course, you're probably renting the property because you'd like to realize a profit. Your property taxes, maintenance, and repairs will not stop just because you've rented the place to somebody else. This means you need to do everything possible to make that rental income worth as much as possible, and making the right insurance decisions will help boost profit you can pocket.

4. Choosing between replacement cost and cash value insurance.

Unless you have full replacement cost, you will only get the amount of money it would cost to fix the repairs needed to bring it to the level it was prior to the loss with depreciation figured in. This could mean you'd be on the hook for a much greater out of pocket expense to have it fixed correctly.

Full replacement cost will cost more, but it won't be as expensive as the out of pocket expense you could face without it.

5. Liability if your tenants or their guests are injured.

Many landlords have a concern about someone being injured on their property. Your tenant will ultimately be responsible for injuries which are caused by their careless or negligence. If a guest falls in the shower, your tenant will be liable, so it's a good idea to make him aware of this risk.

Discuss possible accident scenarios with your insurer as there are some gray areas you'll want to understand thoroughly. For example, if the tenant fails to remove the snow from the front sidewalk and the mailman slips and falls, is it the tenant's responsibility or does it fall back on you, the owner, because the fall didn't happen on or within the structure? It's always better to know as much as you can before an accident happens, and it's never wise to guess or assume when it comes to insurance.

All key issues to address when obtaining insurance can be less worrisome with the right tenants. One of the most important things you can do when renting out a property is easier said than done, but be careful who you rent to. You want somebody who pays the rent, but you also want a tenant who doesn't have a reputation for neglecting their home, making frivolous claims, or having a litigious history.

Once you own three houses, some insurance won't insure any more for you. They don't want the risk. The same for commercial banks. Most of them have a limit on how many houses they will finance.

On the flip side, it is in your best interest not to put your eggs in one basket. If you had 10 mortgages with one bank and you were late (not over 30 days, but let's say 3 weeks because you had a vacancy and were a little tight on cash) your banker would go into a blind panic!

The difference between insurance is like day and night. You will never know how good they are until you file a claim.

Here's a huge mistake I made about deductibles. I thought I would save some money by raising my deductible to

$5,000. We had a hail storm and it did some damage to my roof. I had the insurance company come out and they said it was minor, about $2,500. The roof didn't leak so I let it go at that.

Then we had another hail storm. This one did much more damage, but the roof still didn't leak. I called the insurance company to take a look. He asked for the receipts on the $2,500 damage. I didn't have any. He said the deductible is $5,000 and we will have to add the $2,500 from the previous storm making your deductible $7,500. I thought that was crazy! It takes a lot of net rent to come up with that much money!

I switch to another insurance company. After about a year we had a HUGE hail storm. The new company put on a new roof and paid a $24,000 claim. Since I acted as my own contractor I put 50% of that money in my pocket.

After that lesson here's what I did. I used a different insurance company for every property and lowered my deductible to $2,000. I also used a different mortgage company for each property.

Another hail storm passed through a few years later and I got new roofs on all my properties. Again, because I was able to act as my own contractor (no contractor's license is required in Oklahoma) I was able to have them all put on with no out of pocket expense. Just to make me feel better, I had contractors give me estimates to see how much I saved.

If I had them all insured with one insurance company can you imagine the battle I would have had? It was much easier to deal with individual adjusters and companies.

From my personal experience, USAA is the best, Farmers is in the middle, and Allstate is the bottom of the barrel. This was verified by a friend who is a contractor. When a huge tornado damaged hundreds of homes in Moore, Oklahoma, he was in the middle of all the repair work. He said the difference between insurance companies was like night and day when it came to responding claims.

11. Mistakes when screening tenants

Until you have some hard experience under your belt, you will make mistakes when interviewing tenants. I was no exception.

I have always been in sales. It was in my nature to sell the tenant on renting the place. This was completely wrong. I should have let the tenant sell ME. I should have played the role of a buyer not a seller. Eventually I got smart, but not without some hard lessons.

I remember going to my first landlord's association meeting. When the subject of dealing with tenants came up with one of the guest speakers, the comments from the audience really surprised me. I thought to myself, "these folks are really mean!" It didn't take long before I joined them in their attitude.

For example, I had one couple who came to me in desperation. They were in a lease purchase agreement, they were evicted and lost their $5000 deposit. They had 2 kids with no place to go. They said they had been turned down by landlords over and over again. They were sitting at my kitchen table with tears in their eyes telling me their story.

Stupid me let them move in.

That was the worst 3 years of my life. They had so much junk packed into that house there was hardly enough room to move around. The place looked like a dump. They fought constantly. She would call me up and tell me how stupid her husband was because he spent all the rent money. He would call me up and tell me what a witch she was because she wouldn't give him any of her income for the rent. I drove by the house one day and their son was standing on top of the roof! The neighbors on both sides called me to complain.

The ONLY bright side was the husband was fairly handy and could do quality roofing and carpenter work. I had him work off some of the rent by doing repairs on my other properties.

I finally had enough. I told them they had to move. They hired a lawyer and said they were going to sue me. Can you believe that?

She started quoting me things the lawyer said about the law. She said I had to give her a 90 day notice before evicting them with the lease we had. I never renewed the lease and it had expired after the first year. That was the end of her law suit.

They finally moved and I was left to clean up the mess. I had to rent a huge construction dumpster and I filled it to the top. I had to completely remodel the inside. They destroyed the appliances, the carpets had to be torn out, the walls had to be patched, the place was a total mess.

From that point on I took a whole different approach to interviewing tenants. No more mister "nice guy". I had become on of the audience members whom I previously thought seemed mean.

12. Not listening to your gut

When screening the prospective tenant the most important thing to keep in mind is that you are the person who makes the decision as to whether you want them to move in. Not the other way around.

You always want to use a stall tactic. Even if you are desperate to rent the place and they have a fistful of cash and seem decent enough, stall! Tell them to fill out the application and you will get back with them in 3 days. During that 3 days call their rental references, call their job reference, do a background check, and make sure your husband or wife also interviews them.

You might be thinking, as I did when I first started renting, they look okay, why not take a chance on them?

Remember, you are totally responsible for the hundred-thousand-dollar-plus property you are going to give them access to. You have to pay the mortgage, taxes, insurance, keep up the maintenance, and literally be available for them 24 hours a day, 7 days a week. You want someone who you will be okay dealing with.

Even if you check them out and they are okay, use your common sense when making the final decision. I had one couple who had 7 kids under the age of 10. He had a good job as the manager of a Sonic. Everything looked good on paper. But SEVEN KIDS should have given me a warning signal. I needed to rent the place and he had the deposit and first months rent. So against my gut feeling of SEVEN KIDS COULD BE A PROBLEM I signed the lease and took the money.

For about 6 months everything was going pretty well. Rent was on time, the kids were not causing any problem, she was a pretty good housekeeper. Then it happened. He got in a fight with his boss and quit his job. This is the peak of stupidity. How does someone with seven kids up and quit a job without having another one to go to? He got behind on his rent and couldn't pay. He couldn't find a job and kept telling me about all the interviews he went on.

Answer this question: How do you evict someone with SEVEN LITTLE KIDS? He was 3 months behind on his rent, his utilities were being shut off and his car broke down. Of course, I still had to make the mortgage payment and keep the place up. I finally told him he had to leave and he agreed to go. I had him sign a personal note for the $4,000 he owed me so I could at least take it off my taxes at the end of the year. I knew I would never get paid. I had not reached the point of filing claims in court for money owed to me.

He ended up renting a small house in a low end of town for one-third the rent he was paying me. He got a new job - get this - as a debt collector!

A tenant/landlord relationship is not something you should take lightly. You are entering into a partnership that must be a fair and an equally responsible contract with each party understanding their obligation and what happens if those obligations are not met.

Later, after I learned from my mistake, I was renting the same house. A young couple without any kids looked at it and immediately wanted it. They had the money, they had the income, they looked like really good prospects. They begged me to take the rent and deposit and let them move in immediately. They said their lease was up in two days and they had to move out of their current apartment.

But wait, my gut said, this is too good to be true. I stalled. I told them I would take the application and get back with them in 3 days. I said there was someone ahead of them and they will be letting me know if they want it tomorrow. (I didn't have anyone waiting, and really wanted the rent and deposit - but I was not naive and stupid anymore).

As soon as they filled out the application, I noticed they had different last names. Red flag #1. They had led me to believe they were married. He worked at Target, which seemed pretty good, and he had a good income. Red flag #2. She simply put down "dancer" as her job. Her income was over the top! When I asked her what kind of "dancer" she was, she said she was a stripper at a saloon in a low rent district downtown. The next day I called her and told her someone else had rented the house. Who knows what kind of mess I would have ended up with. Two young, single people, with one of them being a stripper, didn't pass the "smell test", the smell being the parties, booze, and drugs.

Never make the mistake of being in too much of a hurry, no matter how good they look or how bad you need the rent. If you wait, a good tenant will come along. They are out there, you just have to learn how to be patient recognize them.

13. Not cutting the cord mistake

I was called by a law firm asking me if they could look at my rental house. It seemed like a strange request, so I made the appointment.

Two lawyers showed up, a male and female, along with a young girl who was 17 years old. Turns out they were managing the young girl's trust and needed a place for her to live until she turned 18, exactly one year.

The rent seemed like a sure thing. Shouldn't have any problem collecting it from a trust fund. Except for a few parties and the fact that she had two of her friends living with her, everything went along pretty good.

The lease was ready to expire and she asked if she could keep the place and pay me herself. I simply said okay and let her stay. I didn't do any homework about how she was going to pay the rent or where she was going to work. She hadn't worked for the year she lived there.

When the rent was due I had to call her to remind her that she was approaching the late payment date and had to pay. She came up with the money. The second month she couldn't pay and I told her she had to leave.

When I went to the house to get it ready for a new tenant I had the shock of my life. The garage was full of phone books! I mean there was hardly enough room to walk through to the door. She and her friends had contracted with a phone company to deliver phone books in the neighborhood. They all ended up in the garage. I called the phone company and told them to come and pick them up. They refused.

Luckily I had another deadbeat tenant, the one I mentioned earlier who got evicted from their lease-purchase, and had him haul them off to the dump in his truck.

Here is the mistake I made. When I first rented it to the lawyers who were handling the trust fund, I should have asked for a $5,000 deposit, refundable after 90 days, less any rent due after the expiration of the lease, and less any repairs or other expenses. Better yet, I should have asked for a non-refundable deposit of $5,000. They would have paid it.

I also should have made it clear that we are "cutting the cord" when she turns 18 and the lease expires. She must be out on a specific date.

14. Presenting and signing the lease

Signing the lease is the most important part of the entire rental business. You MUST spell everything out verbally with everyone involved present.

Let's say you and I are sitting at the kitchen table and I am presenting you with the lease. Here is what would take place.

1. We verify everything on the application before we go into the lease.

Is your employment still the same?

Is your employer contact information correct?

Is your Social Security number correct?

The Social Security number is really important. If you have to file a law suit or get a judgement for unpaid rent, you are wasting your time if you don't have it.

1. This lease is between (Your tenant's name - both of them if they are a couple) and Bob Oros, Trustee of the Fairhill 517 Land Trust. (Make it clear that you are only the trustee and not the owner.) The lease is for one year, from September 1, 2020, to August 31, 2021.

Your tenant does not need to know that you are the sole owner of the property. This can save you a lot of negotiating headaches later on if they should arise. "I brought up your situation before the "Board of Trustees" and they agreed that you must vacate the property. They are not willing to give you a reduced rent."

If they think you have a lot of property in your name and something goes wrong, they will take advantage of you. When they don't know how many properties you have they are less likely to bring up some kind of law suit. If they know you own 8 or 10 houses they see you as a target.

2. The rent is $1500 per month due on the first day of the month. If paid after midnight on the 5th day of the month there is a $100 late fee applied. If not paid by the 15th, an eviction notice will be filed with the court. The sheriff will serve you with the notice to vacate and you will either leave or be physically removed from the property.

This is where you explain to the tenants that the "Owners of the trust" require you to explain this in the event that something happens in the future that makes it necessary to terminate the lease. You can tell them, "This eviction is filed without you knowing until the sheriff shows up on your door with the notice to vacate the property."

3. The deposit of $1500 was received and will be returned 45 days after the expiration of the lease less any repairs, other than normal wear and tear, that will be necessary to make. If the lease is broken, the deposit is not returned. The deposit is NOT considered the last month's rent. If you leave the property and any rent remains unpaid, a collection notice will be filed with the court and turned over to a collection agency.

I know this seems a little harsh, but remember, it's not you that is being harsh, it is the owners of the trust who are insisting that you, the Trustee, fully explain what happens if the lease agreement is broken.

Why 45 days? This will give you enough time to get a new deposit and not have to take the money out of the bank and give it back to them.

4. All utilities must be in service during the term of this lease.

I used to ride by all my properties after dark on "shut off" day to see if the light were on. If a place was dark, I investigated.

5. A notice to vacate is required by the tenant 30 days prior to the expiration of the lease. If you wish to have your deposit returned, you must give your notice on August 1, 2021. Any later than that and you lose your deposit.

"If you come to me you on the last day of the lease and say your are leaving, your deposit is not returned."

6. No other person to occupy the leased premise without notification.

If they have people move in and they do not let you know and put their name on the lease, at the end of the lease the deposit is considered rent for the additional person.

7. Tenant shall not assign or sub-lease the property.

8. Tenant shall not conduct any business deemed hazardous.

9. Structural alterations or painting will result in loss of deposit. This includes no above ground swimming pools.

10. Bedbugs are totally the responsibility of the tenant.

When they moved into the house, there were no bed bug. The house was thoroughly treated for all types of bugs, including bed bugs.

I had one divorced single mom tenant whose daughter went to Disney World with her x-husband. When she returned she brought bed bugs back with her. The place became infested and she called me to see what I would do. I told her the bed bugs were her problem. She called a pest control company and they said it would cost $1,950 to get rid of them. She told me about it and I called a friend who was in the pest control business. He charged her $850. He had to come back three times to get rid of them. She paid, not me.

11. Hanging pictures, mirrors and other decorations is fine.

12. This is a non-smoking rental agreement.

13. No pets allowed.

14. Please call anytime for maintenance issues.

15. Utilities are currently on. Utilities to be put in your name effective the day you move in.

Page 2 of the lease.

Okay, this is kind of gutsy. I included this with questionable tenants. Even if I did a background check, but they still seemed a little questionable. However, if you have a problem, you will be glad you included it.

Eviction Process & Fees

(1) When rent is not paid by the 5th of the Month, you will receive a District Court Notice: NOTICE TO QUIT-FIVE DAYS—Title 41 O.S., Sec. 6, 7, 1971. This notice will be certified mailed to you and the cost will be $5.00 charged to your account.

(2) When you receive the 5 day notice you now have 5 days to pay ALL your rent that is due in full. If you don't pay your rent within those 5 days we are required to file a 'Forcible Entry & Detainer' at the Oklahoma District Courthouse. You will be charged $105.00 court document processing fees which included AC01-Clerk Fees, AC23-Law Library Fee, AC64-Dispute.

Mediation Fees, and handling fees.

(3) You will now have a court date and you will be served legal papers from a licensed Oklahoma Judicial Process Server. The fee is $50.00.

(4) At the Oklahoma District Courthouse on the date you are scheduled the hearing and judgment will be entered. A verdict will be awarded for non payment of rents that are due. The court fees are $215.70. Fees are AC-01 Clerk Fees, AC08-Sheriff Fees, AC31-Court Clerk Revolving Fund, AC58-Court Appointed Special Advocates, AC59-Council on Judicial Complaints Revolving Fund, AC79-OCIS Revolving Fund, and handling fees.

(5) You have 48 hours to vacate the premises before the Sheriff walks delinquent tenant(s) off the property and changes the locks. The fee to have Oklahoma County Sheriff to walk tenant(s) of the property is $150.00 with handling fees.

At any time you can stop the eviction process by contacting your landlord, Bob Oros, 405-751-9191 to arrange payment.

$5.00 Certificate Mailing of 5 Day Eviction Notice

$105.00 Court Filing Fee

$50.00 Process Server Fee

$215.70 Oklahoma District Courthouse Fee

$150.00 Oklahoma County Sheriff Fee

_____

$525.70 Total for Legal Eviction Fees

+ All Rent Monies and late fees will be entered into a judgment in your name.

Note: I know this is harsh. Sounds like a tough way to start a relationship. I jokingly call it the "prenuptial agreement".

15. Telling the tenant too much.

As discussed in the lease question, it is easy to want to become friends with the tenant. You may like to brag a little and tell them about the properties you have and about how important you are. Resist the temptation. Don't let your ego dictate the conversation. It is much better to let them think you are merely the Trustee.

As I mentioned, in my other life I have always been in sales. My job was always to get people to like and respect me. I had to make them trust me so they would buy from me. Being a landlord really gave me a good balance. I had to force myself to keep my mouth shut. To let them sell me.

Everything you tell a tenant can be turned against you at some future time. They are not your friends, they are not your customers, they are your tenants. It is their job to make you like them. It is their job to sell you on the idea that you will let them continue living in your property.

If you are new to the business and you think this is being a little arrogant. Let's hold judgement and talk again after you have 10 tenant turns under your belt. If you are a seasoned landlord, you know exactly what I am talking about.

I felt the same way when I started, however, now I could write an entire book with the title "Why I Can't Pay My Rent!"

16. Little cats and small dogs.

"But my dog is really small. She is quiet and very well behaved!"

I understand how pets can become part of your family. I have had pets in my life and I know how attached you get to them. However, the truth is, people don't pick up after their tiny dog or cute little cat.

I had a 1200 square foot house that was fixed up really nice. It had a lot of cedar wood, cedar beams in the living room that I had put in, carpets in the bedrooms, plus an outdoor patio that I had filled in with cement to make it maintenance free. No grass to cut.

A salesman for the local newspaper moved into the area and needed a place to live. He really liked my place and asked if it was okay for his wife's two small cats to live with them. I thought, what harm can two small cats cause.

Turned out that he had 4 HUGE cats. He stayed for about 8 months and got transferred. He lost his deposit, but that no where near made up for the damage the cats did. Scratches everywhere. You cannot imagine how much hair four cats will shed in an 8 month period. There was cat hair EVERYWHERE. Even on the cedar beams in the living room.

It took hours and hours trying to get the cat hair out of the place. I have long since sold the it, but I bet you could still find cat hair somewhere hiding in the corners.

I still didn't learn my lesson. A single woman with two French poodles moved in. She left them out in the fenced-in patio area all day while she worked. Of course, she didn't pick up after them. The entire patio was covered with dog shit. I will never forget, I was having some work done on the outside AC unit. The serviceman needed to have another person bring him something. He was describing the location as the second person had been there before. "Oh, you mean the place with all the dog shit on the patio!"

If that wasn't enough, in another one of my rentals I gave in and let a woman rent it with two small dogs. There was a back yard, but she only let them out for a short time during the evening. The rest of the time she kept them locked up in a small sun room off the living room. She was there for a couple of years and when she left we went in to inspect.

The smell almost knocked us over. We scrubbed and scrubbed and simply could not get the smell to go away. Finally I bought 5 gallons of vinegar, poured it all over the floor and let it soak into the walls. I let it set there a couple of days and the smell finally went away.

Finally I learned my lesson. As it said on the lease - no pets. Or so I thought.

Another tenant agreed with the no pet rule and said he didn't have a dog or cat. He didn't consider a "small lizard" a pet. By the time he moved out the thing was 2 feet long and occupied an entire bedroom in the house! Now I learned my lesson - right down to the bone. I tell this story when explaining my no pet rule on the lease.

17. When they move out

It's easy to have high hopes when you sign the lease and your new tenants start moving in. However, when they move out, you see who they really are. This is not meant to discourage you, but rather to prepare for it by knowing what you will have to deal with.

For the most part, tenants don't clean. After a year or two they move out and you go in to assess the place. What will you find?

18 Tenants don't dust.

The first thing you will notice is the ceiling fans. Dust will be hanging off and they will require some heavy duty cleaning. It is normal that when someone moves out of a house that there will be a lot of dust and dirt. But, because they are moving out of a "rental" there will be more. I guess it's the same reason you don't wash a rental car when returning it.

19. Tenants don't change light bulbs.

At least half the light bulbs will be burned out. For some reason they don't seem to mind sitting in a room with half the light. I tried buying the long-life bulbs, but they would turn up missing. I know, hard to believe.

It's a good idea to stay away from fancy light fixtures that need special bulbs. Especially in the bathroom. Because that is the one place they will not sacrifice light. A dim light in the bathroom, or a burned out bulb, will trigger a maintenance call. They have to be able to see to put their makeup on. With a fancy light fixture you will end up spending a Saturday afternoon trying to figure out how to replace the bulb. The main rule is to keep it simple and be consistent. I'm talking SUPER SIMPLE.

20. Tenants don't clean appliances.

The oven and the microwave will be caked with grease and grime. Even if you have a self-cleaning oven, they will never use it. A stove and microwave are not too expensive. There is a point where it is easier to simply buy new ones and get rid of the old ones. The same goes for the dishwasher. I got so good I could replace a dishwasher in 30 minutes. A garbage disposal in about 15 minutes. I always left it up to the tenant to furnish a refrigerator, washer and dryer.

If you provide a refrigerator, washer and dryer, you are responsible for fixing them if they stop working. However, I always insisted on hooking them up for the new tenant. If you leave it up to them I guarantee you it will end up leaking and causing a mold problem.

I had one tenant buy a new cloths dryer. She had it delivered, plugged it in, used it for two years and never hooked up the vent. The area behind the dryer was a total mess filled with lint and mold. That's why it's a good idea to hook it up for them, or at least inspect it the next time you are spraying for bugs or changing the air filter.

21. Tenants don't clean carpets.

The carpet will be disgusting. It will smell, have stains and be in terrible shape. One of the first things I did when I started renting property is learn how to lay tile floors. At one point I had 10 houses and did not have a single square foot of carpet in any of them. A tile floor will withstand about anything.

It's easier than you think. Have someone who knows how to do it help you with the first one. After that, buy a tile saw and give it a try yourself. I got so good at it I could even tile counter tops and make them look fantastic! You can buy a filament that glues down to the old laminated counter top and makes it possible to put the tile right over it. If you have to hire someone to do it you will go broke.

22. Smoke alarms and air filters.

Tenants don't replace batteries or air filters. When the smoke alarm starts to beep with a low battery signal a tenant will simply take the low battery out and throw it away. If you leave it up to the tenant to change the air filters, it will never get done.

The solution to both of these is to do it yourself. Changing the air filter every 90 days will give you a chance to inspect the property. Replacing all the smoke alarm batteries during the month of January will make sure it gets done plus gives you the opportunity to inspect the furnace as well and the entire house.

You don't want to have a fire and the inspector discovers you don't have working smoke detectors. Another important thing is to put a CO_2 detector near the furnace. The possibility that a child could die from CO_2 escaping from a faulty furnace is a scary thought.

23. Tenants don't spray for bugs.

You can buy commercial grade bug spray on Amazon that works as good as the pest control companies use. A good habit to get into is schedule a visit every 90 days to change the air filter and spray for bugs. These double as inspections and you never know what you will find. I discovered a tenant was making meth in one of my rentals. Had I not done inspections every 90 days it might have gone on for years! I immediately evicted the tenants.

24. Tenants don't know how to paint.

Many times tenants will ask it they can paint the walls a different color. You will notice in the lease that it says, "If you paint, you lose your deposit." If you have to repaint over a tenant's paint job you will understand why. They don't have a clue about doing it correctly. Even if they say they are really good at it and know how to do a professional paint job. They don't.

I had one tenant paint the bedroom dark purple. Even the ceiling was dark purple. On top of that, she painted a doorway on one of the walls. It was supposed to represent a doorway to a spiritual world! She got paint all over the woodwork (they didn't know you are supposed to tape it off.) They got paint on the ceiling fan, vent covers, as well as the sliding glass door. It took days to get that room back in shape when it should have taken an hour.

For economical reasons I painted all the walls in every property the exact same color. It was a carefully selected beige color that would go with just about anything. I used the highest quality paint I could buy at Home Depot. When I went in to prepare the property I could roll the entire house in a matter of hours. I never had to cut in or tape off the woodwork except for the first time I painted it. I also never had to worry about trying to match the color. In the rental complexes they have a paint called landlord white. I took the cue and found my own landlord beige.

Being consistent in as many ways as possible is a huge money and time saver. Every light bulb in every house was a 60 watt bright white (daylight) bulb. I bought them by the case.

I kept air filters on hand in my garage at all times. Just by luck, all my furnaces used the same size.

I used the same tile on all my floors. If I had to replace a broken or damaged tile, no problem, I had plenty in the "rental" area of my garage.

I had a commercial size bug sprayer that I kept full with the commercial quality bug spray I used. I never had a termite problem and I believe I may have prevented it by my consistent spraying. I sprayed both inside and outside and always applied double what a pest control would use.

I used the same style shingle on all my roofs. If I had to make a repair, I had some on hand. I also had the roofing tar on hand in the event I drove by and noticed a shingle had blown off.

The outside of all my properties were mostly brick, however they all had an area that was painted. They were all painted light grey. I never had to match the paint and I always had some on hand to do touch up.

I have every tool I need to do anything. Plumbing, electrical, carpenter, as well as tools to lay tile.

25. Tenants don't mow the lawn.

You want your property to look good. Keeping the lawn mowed is a big part of it. I can drive down any street and tell who are owners and who are renters simply by looking at the lawn. They will never trim the bushes, never edge, and when they do mow, they will never bag the grass. And since they wait until the lawn looks like a field, there are clumps of grass all over the lawn. It looks terrible.

On one occasion I had a duplex and a neighbor from across the street called the police because the two tenants were fighting over whose turn it was to mow the lawn. An arrangement they set up on their own.

After that, I found Jose, a guy that was mowing lawns in the neighborhood. He gave me an excellent price and I used him for years (I still do). He was worth every penny. He also trimmed my trees when needed, cleaned my gutters as well as raked up all the leaves in the springtime.

But still, I used to toy with the idea of doing the lawn maintenance myself. However, when the temperature reaches 90 or 100 degrees in the summer, it was really much easier to pay Jose and his crew to do it. But I still cringed when I paid him, thinking that if I did it myself, I could keep the money.

26. Tenants lie about their background.

When I first started renting properties I believed everything the prospective tenants told me. As I went along I learned to spot red flags. However, I kept finding things out after they already moved in. Then it was too late.

I had one young couple move into one of my rentals. On the surface they seem perfect. He was a chef and she worked in retail. They had no children and acted very polite. Don't misunderstand, I am happy to rent to families with kids. I took the deposit check and let them move some stuff in the garage before the effective date of the lease. This was a big mistake. This was also before I started taking applications and making them wait 3 days.

I took the check to the bank and there was no money to cover it. They gave me a sad story and finally came up with the cash to cover the check. Then the first month's rent check bounced.

I later discovered that he lost his job and couldn't find another one. He also had two judgements against him, one for $27,000 and another for $125,000. He was driving drunk and ran into someone. She also turned out to be a drunk. Three months later, when I finally got rid of them, they had made the biggest mess of any tenant I ever had. There were enough empty whiskey bottles and beer bottles to stock a huge bar. My lack of judgement cost me about $2,500 in lost rent.

This all could have been avoided by investing $29 in a background check. You can set up an account online and it takes about 2 minutes to enter the tenant's information. You will be able to turn down a potential problem tenant with confidence. No more guess work.

The application doesn't need to be complicated. Here is the basic information you need. If there are two people I have each person fill one out and sign it. Even if they are married and the husband says, "I want to put it in my wife's name". All the more reason to have them both fill one out.

Rental Application

Full Name   _____

Employer   _____

Employer's phone   _____

Annual income   _____

Email   _____

Date of Birth   month ____ day____ year_____

SS Number   _____ - _____ - _____

Current landlord _____

Landlord's phone _____

Rent _____

I agree to a credit/background check.

X_____

27. Tenants will lie about smoking.

The lease says "this is a non-smoking rental agreement." For many tenants, this doesn't matter, they will smoke anyway. I have nothing against smoking, I just don't want to clean up after a tenant when they leave.

If you are a non-smoker, you can tell immediately when you walk in whether they are smoking in the house. For me, it means they just lost their deposit.

Some people think it is okay to smoke in the garage. I had one single man who set up a "man cave" in the garage. He had a TV and a couple of chairs. When he left the smell in the garage was like an ashtray. The ceiling and walls were yellow. It took an unbelievable amount of work to get rid of odor. I had to paint the walls with two coats of KILZ before I could apply a coat of regular paint.

I tell this story when I am signing a lease with a new tenant so the message will be loud and clear.

28. Above ground swimming pools.

I had one tenant call me and ask if I would help her set up an above ground swimming pool that she bought on sale for her kids. When I got there it HUGE. I think the box said 24 feet across! It was deeper than her kids were tall. This made no sense at all. I talked her into taking it back and buying a little disposable kiddy pool.

This was before I put it in the lease that no above ground swimming pools were allowed.

Five houses up from one of my rentals there was a rental property owned by someone else. The tenants had hired someone to come and dig a big hole in the back yard and fill it with sand to use as a base for an above ground pool. All the sod was removed and piled next to the back driveway. It was a real mess. They had to take down part of the fence to make it fit.

The pool was installed without the owner's knowledge or permission. I used to drive by and the pool was never maintained. The water was green. The grass around the pool was never cut and it was a disaster!

They moved out and the landlord/owner was in the backyard taking down the pool. Not only was it a monumental job to take it down, but repairing the yard was just as much work. This simply reinforced my rule about no above swimming pools.

Below is a swimming pool I built for a home I was living in. I decided to rent the house and had to tear it down. Big mistake. This cost me about $2,500, money I should have spent on tile floors and new windows. By the way, windows are easier than you think to install.

29. Tenants think you are a bank.

When something goes wrong in the life of a tenant, the first thing they do is don't pay the rent. The reason this happens is because it was not made clear when they signed the lease. It must be clear to them that you mean what you say when the 15th of the month rolls around and they are served with an eviction notice.

One of the biggest mistakes I made was being a wimp when it came to sympathizing with a tenant when they had a problem. You have to keep in mind that you are running a business and it is not a bank or charity. Even if they promise to pay the late fee, you are still losing. Unpaid rent is the ultimate dead horse bill. If they go a month without paying, you will never get it. I mean NEVER. You have to nip it in the bud.

I had a tenant who paid their rent on time for more than a year. Her brother died and she had to pay for the funeral. Tenants don't have savings accounts and they usually don't have any credit available on any of their credit cards. So what do they do when they need money. They come to you, the landlord. I can tell you with all the experience and confidence I have - you won't get paid back rent.

Then her grandmother died without any life insurance and she had to pitch in $1500 to pay for her share of the expenses. It was funny how "her share" was the same amount as the rent. She was now into me for a three thousand dollar dead horse bill!

Another month went and she made a partial payment. She was now 3 months behind on her rent. I had to evict her.

If I had been smart (as I later became), I would have evicted her 15 days after she was late. When you let them slide, you are weak. You are not the Salvation Army, or a charity. There are places people can go to get help paying their rent. It is not up to you to finance their problems. You are not even financing them - you are giving them a gift, because you will never see back rent.

Once I got smart, I stopped letting people make their problems MY PROBLEMS. If a family member dies, or someone gets sick, or a dozen other life situations it is up to them to solve their own problems. It's funny. Somehow they always find a way - and they do it without your help. You simply can't get involved. If you do, you will go broke. I know, I know, that sound really tough.

Tenants are a lot like kids. You have to teach them to be self reliant. If you do everything for them and make it easy, they will never learn how to solve problems without you .

Not only that, when a tenant owes you back rent, they get mad at YOU. Early on, I had a tenant who was married with two little kids. He received a monthly check for $1500 from a trust set up by his grandfather to make sure his grandchildren always had a place to live. That's pretty much a guaranteed rent payment. This guy got over his head in consumer debt and after he made all his payments, didn't have enough to pay the rent. He got behind and couldn't pay. Stupid me let him slide. He never got caught up and left owing me $3,000. Not only that, he thought I was the meanest person on the planet. He called me names, sent me nasty text and email messages, and got really obnoxious because I was trying to collect the rent.

I warned him that if anything was missing from the house when he left I would report it to the police. He hit the ceiling! He said, "how dare you accuse me of being a thief!" I said that fact that you are a thief has already been established. You took $3,000 that belongs to me.

They even try to use religion against you. They say "what kind of Christian would put a family out on the street?"

The hard and firm rule it this. If you don't pay - you don't stay. On the 15th an eviction notice is served. Period. That is the way the "board of directors" want it. Now, if any tenant swears at me and calls me names, all I have to do is calmly say, "I will pass your comments along to the board."

30. Deposit red flags to watch for.

Let's say the deposit if $1,500 and the rent is $1,500. If they start off trying to negotiate the deposit payment, for example, I will pay the deposit in two payment, the answer is no.

If they don't have the money to move in, and you work out a payment deal, you have just set a precedent for all future transactions. If you are firm and say you must have the entire amount, it is surprising how they are always able to come up with it. You have also just set a precedent for all future transactions. No negotiating.

I notice many rental properties advertise that the "first and last months rent is required to move in." I am sure there must be some logic behind this, but I just don't get it. When the lease is up all they have to do is walk. You have no recourse if the place is destroyed. You have nothing to hold them accountable. They don't even have to give you a notice. In their mind, the last month is already paid, they are free to vacate.

I always made it clear that the deposit is not the last month's rent, and it will be returned after the property is inspected. Any unusual repairs will be deducted.

I had one tenant leave most of his furniture in the house. There was an old desk in the back bedroom that was so large I had to saw it in two pieces to get it out. He must have brought it in pieces and put it together in the bedroom. I deducted $500 for having to remove all the furniture he left behind.

He had a fit! He thought he was doing me a favor by leaving it. My response, "sorry buddy, I had to pay someone to come and haul it off to the dump. Between the dump fee and the charge for cutting up the desk and removing the rest of the furniture, the cost was $500." Being tough was finally starting to pay off.

31. Renting to the family.

When you rent to a family member you are asking for trouble. Also, you have stepped out the role of being a landlord. Family members expect to be treated different. Regardless of how much upfront talking, negotiating and promising you do, they will still not consider themselves as a tenant. Plus, they will not consider you as their landlord.

If you don't care about learning how to be a successful landlord, and you don't care about making money, then rent to a family member. If you think I am wrong, or I am not being fair to family members who are in need of a place to live, go ahead and do it. In the long run, you will agree with me. I could give you examples, but I can't say anything about any family members or it will come back to me in a bad way.

I am not saying that you cannot rent to a family member. If you have a property, and all you want to do is keep it occupied, no problem. Just don't expect any gratitude or money. You won't get either.

32. Home warranty mistakes.

You might be tempted to get a home warranty to protect you from expensive repairs. Don't do it. As soon as you call them with a problem you will find out why.

At one point I thought a home warranty on my rental properties would be a great thing. I signed up five properties on a plan. At the time it was $40 per month for each property. I had three issues before I told them to take their warranties and stick it.

I was naive enough to think they would send out high quality service people to make the repair. I was 100% wrong. They send out their dumbest rookies. Why, because it is a sure thing for the service company. You are not the customer, the home warranty company is. The only reason they got the contract was because they were the lowest bidder. And when these low-end service providers discover that most customers don't complain, the figure it's easy money.

I had a plugged toilet. They sent out some 19 year old kid with a hand-tool from Home Depot. He fiddled around for about 10 minutes and said he couldn't fix it.

I told him to get out of the way. I unbolted the toilet from the floor, picked up the toilet and discovered there was a root that had grown into the drain. I cut it out and put the toilet back. I told the kid to get lost. They charged me $125 for the service call.

I had a tenant call me and said he had a "hot spot" on his bedroom floor. I called the home warranty company. They sent some goofball out to take a look. He said whatever it is it is not covered by your contract. He left and they sent me a service call bill for $125.

I went to the equipment rental company, rented a cement saw and cut a hole in the slab about 2 feet by 2 feet. The hot water pipe going from the hot water heater to the bathroom had a leak. I repaired the leak, filled it in with a couple bags of sand, topped it off with a couple bags of cement and the problem was solved.

Don't let these types of problems scare you. You can do more than you think you can. It is always good to have someone you know who will guide you through these situations.

Being a landlord is an ongoing learning experience. You never know what to expect. That's the fun of it. If you let these things get you down, you might not be cut out to be "the real estate investment" business. You have to say to yourself, "no problem - I can pretty much fix anything - and if I can't, I can find someone who can!"

I could go on with a few more example, but you get the picture. Home warranty companies have to be the biggest scam going. On my personal home, if something breaks, I go to Lowes or Home Depot and buy a new one.

My refrigerator stopped cooling a while ago. I worked on it for about an hour, watched a couple of YouTube videos and decided to go buy a new one. They had some great looking, brand new refrigerators on sale for less than a thousand dollars. I bought one, they delivered it the next day, carried off my old one and problem solved. My wife loves the new one and I am a hero. The same thing happened with my dryer. Appliances wear out. Warranty companies will not replace them unless they are completely gone. I'm talking dead!

The only two things I don't mess with too much is the heat and air system and the garage doors. I have a good person for each of these that I can call and depend on them for an honest repair. This is especially important for a heat and air company. They are pretty much a bunch of crooks. They even have seminars that teach them how take advantage of people by selling new units rather than repair the old ones.

Garage doors are dangerous. I know of one guy that was trying to install and tighten the spring. The thing snapped and the screwdriver went flying right into his head. Killed him instantly. That's why I have a professional repair my garage doors.

On your heat and air units, regular maintenance is important. Keep the filter clean and hose out the compressor unit at least every six month. That alone will save you a ton of repairs.

33. Responding to maintenance calls.

Let me remind you again about the location of your rental properties. Buy them close to your home.

It's always a good idea to encourage your tenants to call you regardless of how small the issue seems. Get there as soon as you can to see what is going on. A tiny leak under the kitchen sink and cause a huge amount of water damage on the entire area.

Whenever I had a problem with a faucet leaking under the sink I always took the time to replace the entire unit with a Delta faucet. Once you see how easy they are to install you will be happy to pay a little more for them. Plus, all Delta products have a lifetime guarantee.

The same goes for the toilet. They are easy to replace and not very expensive. Delta has a great line of toilets called "power flush" that work great. I have three of them in my home.

Ceiling fans are another thing that are very easy to replace and they make a huge difference. I must have installed 50 or more fans over my tenure as a landlord. A tenant can't do too much damage to a ceiling fan so you can buy something with a little quality to it. When possible, I like to install the ones that attach directly to the ceiling rather that the kind that hand on a rod. The ones that hang take longer to balance than they do to install.

34. Why not just hire a handyman?

You need 10 rental houses before it makes any sense to hire someone to do all your repairs. If you don't do it yourself, you will not be learning anything, and you will be giving up all your profit. If you do everything right, you can quit your day job and become your own full time handyman with 10 houses. While you are buying and managing them you are getting an education that you can't get anywhere else at any price. You are in it by yourself for yourself. It is the ultimate independence. You can do it.

35. What about a management company?

This is a great idea once your rental properties are generating enough income.

If this is something you are interested in there is only one that I would recommend. It is owned and managed by Scott Nachatilo, OKC Home Realty Services, LLC. Their phone number is 405-232-5800. He has a program for every size investor.

For a ton of helpful information visit his website at: https://www.yourokcpropertymanager.com/

If you decide to go this route, it can be the most important relationship you develop in your entire investment career. Even if you are reading this and you live anywhere in the country, go to Scott's website and gather all the information he has so generously posted. You can also use his business and a way to measure your local property manager.

36. When to refinance?

I have always had a dilemma about the length of the mortgage. I always needed as much cash flow as I could get so I opted for the 30 year mortgage. This was great for the short term, but for the long term, it was a mistake. Fifteen years go by mighty fast. And your equity goes up just a fast. You are not only making money on the appreciation, but making money by having the tenants pay off your mortgage.

If you had 10 houses with 15 year mortgages on all of them, and you broke even every month as far as your cash flow goes, you would still be getting rich. If the houses were at least $100,000 each in value, you could be a millionaire in 15 years or less. If your mortgages were all 30 years, you have a lot longer to go before you can cash out, if that is your goal.

If you are 25 years old, and you need the lowest mortgage payment you can get, a 30 year might be your best choice. However, you still have the option to refinance later on and opt for a 15 year mortgage. As the rents go up you might be able to swing a shorter mortgage term and accumulate equity at a faster rate.

On the other hand, if you are 55 years old and just starting out, you might want to opt for the 15 year mortgage.

As you can see, it is both a personal and financial decision. I made some financing mistakes that I could have avoided if I had been smarter. But I came out okay in spite of some of my dumb moves.

Refinancing has many pros and conns. I bought my first two properties by simply taking over the mortgage. They were both rental properties and the owners had moved out of state. I knew they were having a hard time managing a rental from another state so I sent them a letter and said I could be the solution to their problem. I offered to take over their property for the balance of their mortgage. The area was having a hard time and prices had gone down. I ended up buying them both. After about 3 years things turned around, as they always do, and I refinanced them. I had acquired enough equity to get an 80% loan and take out enough cash to put a 20% down payment on a third property.

I could have simply kept them, paid off the mortgages and owned them free and clear. If I never made another real estate investment I would still have made out pretty good. The rent kept going up and up. However, I had a goal of 10 properties. Whether or not to refinance and reinvest the equity really depends on your personal goals.

37. How to sell - this is important

Here are the steps I recommend you take when selling a rental property. This is going to be a lot different than you will hear anywhere else. I had to learn these things the hard way and a lot of unnecessary lost money.

1. Get an appraisal. Even though this more than likely can't be used by the bank when the buyer gets financing, it will give you an exact price and remove all the guesswork and mystery when presenting your asking price.

Be sure the appraiser gets a correct measurement of the square feet. You absolutely cannot rely on the tax appraisal for the correct square feet.

Since this is not a bank appraisal you might be able to get a discount on the appraisal fee. This appraisal is going to be part of your presentation to potential buyers. There is no guesswork and no negotiating.

2. Establish your selling price. Let's say your property appraised at $150,000. You have the comps provided by the appraiser to go along with your property presentation. Reduce the price by 6%, the commission you would normally pay a realtor. Your selling price is $141,000. This price is an "as is" price. This is really important so let me say that again. This is an "as is" price. If the buyer wants to hire an inspector, you are under no obligation what-so-ever to make any of the repairs. If they do spend money on an inspection, you can rest easy, because you are selling the house "as is". Let's say they do hire an inspector and they find that the outside AC unit is in need of replacement. You say, "fine, that is why the price is reduced by $9,000." No matter what an inspector finds, no problem - same answer.

You are in control of the sale. This kind of deal drives a real estate agent crazy if there is one involved. THEY want to be in control.

3. What if a real estate broker brings in a buyer? That's fine, but with a broker, the price is now 3% higher to cover the commission. So the selling price just went up by $4,500. This is spelled out clearly in your presentation.

If the buyer wants you to pay $2000 towards closing cost, no problem, add it to the selling price. Regardless of what they come up with, simply add it to the price for a maximum of $150,000, the appraised price.

You can see how this takes all the negotiating out of the deal and you are 100% protected. No typical seller worries.

Selling price $141,000 "as is" - see appraisal.
Selling price with a broker +3%= $145,500.
Selling price with $2,000 closing cost = $147,500.

Even with a broker and with $2,000 going towards closing cost the buyer is still buying it for $2,500 under the appraised value.

What you have done is eliminate all the games real estate people play in order to justify their commission.

If they bring a broker, he or she can fill out the contract. If not, you can send them to your prearranged mortgage broker and they can fill out the contract.

All the information for your mortgage broker is included in your presentation.

Warning. What ever you do - DO NOT sign a listing agreement with a broker. All you need to do is list your property as a "for sale by owner" on Zillow. When you receive 10 to 15 calls from hungry brokers, tell them to bring you a buyer and you will pay them 3%. They will make an appointment and try to talk you into signing an exclusive. If you do fall for the trap, you have just given them a free ticket to 3% of the gross sales amount for doing nothing but put it on the MLS listing.

The advertised price is $150,000. When they come to look at the place, show them your presentation with all the above included. It's a great deal for the buyer, it's a stress free deal for you the seller, and for the broker, it's an easy 3%.

If the stars are all lined up, and a buyer comes in without a broker, you can be sure, they will buy it if it meets their requirements. I would MUCH rather give the broker's 6% commission to the new owner than to pay it to a real estate broker for doing practically nothing.

It is my prediction that the real estate sales business will become so competitive because of the internet and how easy it is to sell a house yourself, that many of them will go by the wayside because of the nature of the business. They are simply not needed.

Selling to a tenant.

Every once in a while a tenant asks if they can buy the house. If you say no, their attitude towards the house will change. They will take better care of it if they think there is a possibility they can buy it. Here is my solution to the problem. I tell them I will consider selling. I give them a copy of this, with the numbers adjusted for their situation. Only one person ever bought the house they were living in.

1. Debt ratio... Evidence from studies of mortgage loans suggest that borrowers with a higher debt-to-income ratio are more likely to run into trouble making monthly payments. The 43 percent debt-to-income ratio is important because, in most cases, that is the highest ratio a borrower can have and still get a Qualified Mortgage. To calculate your debt-to-income ratio, you add up all your monthly debt payments and divide them by your gross monthly income. Your gross monthly income is generally the amount of money you have earned before your taxes and other deductions are taken out. All bills (rent-car-installments) _____ divided by gross income _____ – debt ratio _____%

2. Job history... When determining your ability to pay (and therefore determining how much house you can afford), a lender will calculate your average income based on your pay from the past 24 months. It's pretty straightforward if you've had the same job and same income and pay structure, but if any of those things changed in the past two years — or will change soon, you may face challenges when trying to get a mortgage.

3. Credit score... With a conventional loan for a house that's backed by Fannie Mae or Freddie Mac, for example, the minimum score required is set at 620. But the lowest credit score to buy a house with an FHA loan is 580. Keep in mind, however, that individual lenders may raise the bar higher based on other factors, such as your income or how much of a down payment you're putting down. That also affects your interest rates. As a generalization, the average credit score to buy a house is 600 or above.

4. Down payment... FHA loans (mortgages insured by the Federal Housing Administration) require a down payment of at least 3.5 percent. Depending on your credit history, the type of dwelling and your reason for buying, the minimum down payment could be 5 percent or more. $5,000 to $7,000 for a down payment would work.

5. **Mortgage**... The current average 30-year fixed mortgage rate in Oklahoma remained stable at 4.43%.

6. **Estimated monthly payment...** Mortgage principle and interest would be about 775. Taxes and insurance about 450. Total payment about 1225.

38. How to advertise a for sale by owner.

Once you have your appraisal done and copies of your presentation ready, all you have to do is go to Home Depot and buy a For Sale By Owner sign. Post it on the front lawn. put a few small signs at the entrance of the addition, or at the end of the street. Take some inside pictures and post your listing on Zillow. That's it.

When you sell or rent, you need a list of features. Here's an example:

EDMOND HOME FOR LEASE 1475 MONTH
801 NW 140th Street, Edmond, OK 73013 -
Call Bob at 405-719-9191

Lawn service included (you don't need a mower).

All tile floors (you don't need a vacuum).

24/7 Maintenance (you don't need a tool box).

Energy efficient (new windows-new roof-5 new ceiling fans)

~ 3 Bedroom 2 bath

~ Mud room

~ Large storage closet

~ In home green house

~ Built-in countertop stove

~ New dishwasher

~ Huge shower in master bedroom

~ 2 car garage

~ Large back yard w/gazebo

~ Laundry room w/d hookup

~ Entertainment center up to 80" TV

~ Very private and secure

~ Excellent neighborhood

~ close to shopping, movies, restaurants

~ easy access to John Kilpatrick turnpike

~ Edmond schools:

  - elementary-Charles Haskell

  - middle-Summit

  - high school-Santa Fe

Sorry, no section 8, no pets and no smoking
(this is a very nice place to live for 1475 per month).

Note about section 8. I only rented to a section tenant once. Once was enough. This is a specialized area of the rental business. Unless you know what you are doing, I strongly advise against it. I have only heard nightmares about dealing with section 8 tenants.

39. Mistakes when selling a property.

Hiring a broker to list your property. With the availability of the internet and websites like Zillow, you don't need to pay an additional 3% for someone to list your property. Once again, don't let them talk you into an exclusive listing. If I have repeated myself on this point, it is because it is really important.

40. When to sell

That depends on your personal situation.

If you have 10 properties that are making a good net profit, you might want to hire a management company to take care of them and never sell. However, you want to have someone to pass the property to when you die with a trust all set up. You certainly don't want to leave a mess for your spouse to clean up should you die first.

If you have less than 10, let's say 5 or 6, and they all have mortgages on them, you might want to pick your favorite one or two, sell the others and pay off the mortgages. You have just tripled your Social Security check and eliminated much of your headache. If you are reaching an age where you don't want to be bothered with tenant headaches, this might be a good option.

Let's be realistic. Let's say you have 8 properties worth over one million dollars. Sounds pretty impressive. However, you have 16 toilets that could plug up, 8 roofs that could leak, 16 skylights that could get blown out by a hail storm, 8 AC compressors that could go out on a hot summer night at about $3,000 each, 8 heating units that could go out on a cold night, 8 garage doors that won't work, and 8 termite possibilities, to mention just a few.

It's 2:00 AM, 100 degrees, the phone rings, the caller ID says its one of your tenants, they are letting you know the AC isn't cooling, how do you respond? If you are young and eager to take on the challenge, all is good. However, if you are retired and want to enjoy a peaceful nights sleep, that's a whole different story.

Don't forget, when a tenant loses their job it becomes YOUR problem. They can also skip out without paying the rent, or you could have two vacancies and have trouble meeting all your expenses. As a landlord you are dealing with some pretty low end folks. The kind that like to blame you for their problems. Not to say there are not some really nice folks who are renters, and I hope you are lucky enough to find the.

So the question of when to sell depends on your age and your tolerance level.

If I had it to do over again I might consider doing this:.

I would take a closer look at my wife's and my personal qualities. We are both as neat as a pin. Every house we have ever lived in was always kept up in prime condition. When it comes to keeping a place clean, very few people could equal my wife. When it comes to doing home remodeling and repairs, few people can equal me.

If we wanted to sell our house all we would have to do is put up a sign. It is literally always ready to show. We have absolutely no junk and we don't keep anything we don't need. As I said, I can do any type of repair or remodel you can think of. Even though I was self employed with an unsteady income, I still had pretty good credit.

Taking the above into account, I would have bought a starter home, repair and remodel it, sell it and upgrade to a bigger home. Do it again and again. Over the same 30 year period I could have ended up with a million dollar plus home, sold it without having to pay capital gains tax, bought a cottage on a lake somewhere, or buy an RV, and retired with an MBA. Massive Bank Account.

I ended up pretty much the same, however, instead of going in a straight line, I was like a sail boat tacking into the wind. Back and forth with slow progress and many mistakes along the way.

There are few things in life that can give the rush of owning rental properties. It seems like you go along day to day solving problems, taking care of maintenance issues, collecting rent, looking for another property to buy, laying awake at night worrying about what AC unit or what furnace will stop working, having your heart skip a beat every time your caller ID says one of your tenants, then it happens.

You start figuring out how fast your mortgages are being paid down every month. Much more than you could ever save out of your paycheck. Then you look at the house prices. They are going up 4 or 5 percent.

Then you realize that the 4 or 5 percent is on the gross value of the house! That means that on a $150,000 house, your increase is $7,500. Your total equity is $35,000. Wait, can that be right? I am getting over 25% return on my equity!

You say to yourself, I have 5 houses. My total equity has grown to $175,000. My appreciation alone is $37,500 a year.

My mortgages are being paid down $2,400 per year on each property! That's a total of another $12,000 per year!

You begin thinking; "All 5 of my houses are rented and paying expenses with a positive cash flow of $300 per month per house. Yikes, can that be? That's $10,800 positive cash flow per house. For my 5 houses that is $54,000 per year positive cash flow. The total assets of my 5 houses are $750,000."

"Hmmm... $54,000 cash flow

$37,000 appreciatIon

$12,000 mortgage reduction

$103,000 per year income"

"From 5 houses! Just think if I doubled that to 10 houses! All I have to do is become a skilled landlord and avoid all the mistakes Bob has laid out here for me. Life is good!"

My hope for you is this:

That you make a lot of money and avoid some of the costly mistakes I made. My goal is to sell enough copies of this book to recover the losses I made over the years. You can help. If you have enjoyed the "confessions" I made in this book, leave a good comment or review at the place you bought it. Also recommend it to your colleagues so we can all be better at what we do.

Wishing you all the best,

Bob Onos

Below are more books by Bob Oros

For information visit www.BobOros.com

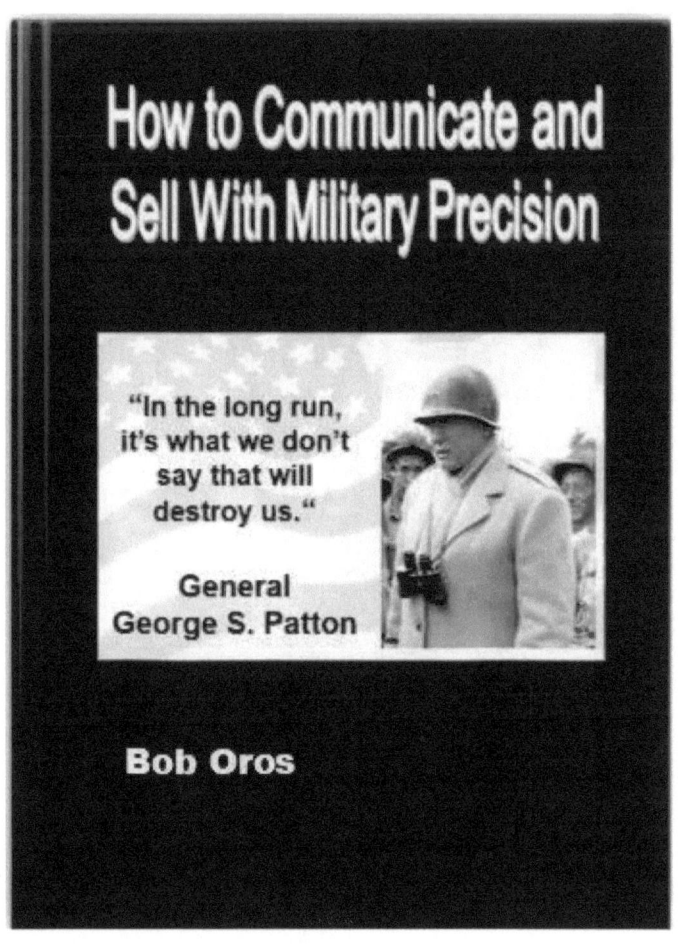

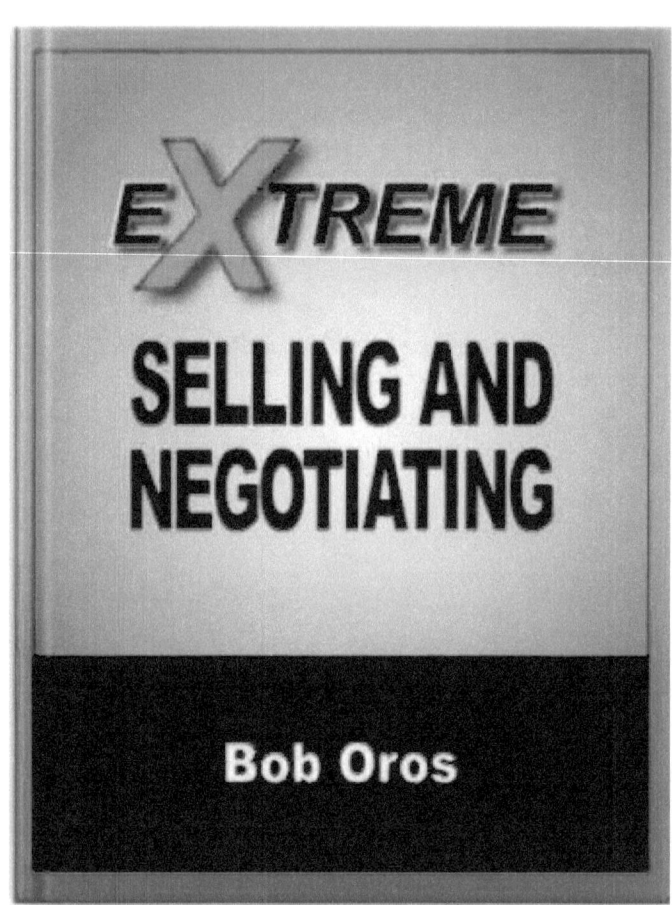

EXTREME

SELLING AND NEGOTIATING

Bob Oros

29 REASONS
You Don't Make The Sale
And a Solution for All of Them

Bob Oros

IF YOU DON'T ASK
Close The Sale and Get Paid

Bob Oros

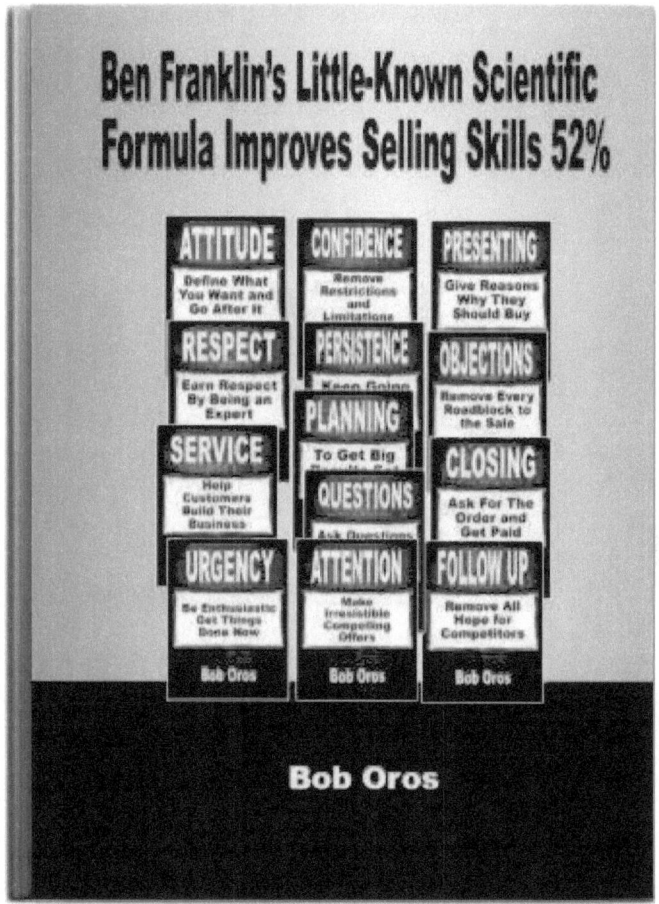

A MORE CONFIDENT SALES PERSON

Bob Oros

NEGOTIATING
YOUR BEST PRICE

It not only takes a superior product
to succeed, it also takes the ability
to negotiate a price that buyers, like
those pictured above, can live with.

Bob Oros

HOW TO MASTER THE ART AND SCIENCE OF SELLING

Bob Oros

www.ingramcontent.com/pod-product-compliance
Lightning Source LLC
Chambersburg PA
CBHW021440210526
45463CB00002B/586